Beneath a Morphine Moon

by Traci Siler

Mijikai Press

Copyright © 2014 by Traci Siler

All rights reserved. This book or any portion thereof may not be reproduced or used in any manner whatsoever without the express written permission of the publisher except for the use of brief quotations in a book review.

Printed in the United States of America
First Printing, 2014
ISBN 0692254803

Mijikai Press
2901 Old Orchard Road
Raleigh, NC 27607

www.facebook.com/MijikaiPress

dedicated to Fellow West Nile Survivors

In September 2012, Traci Siler was bitten by a mosquito at a baseball game near her home in Texas and contracted West Nile Virus. Her life has not been the same since.

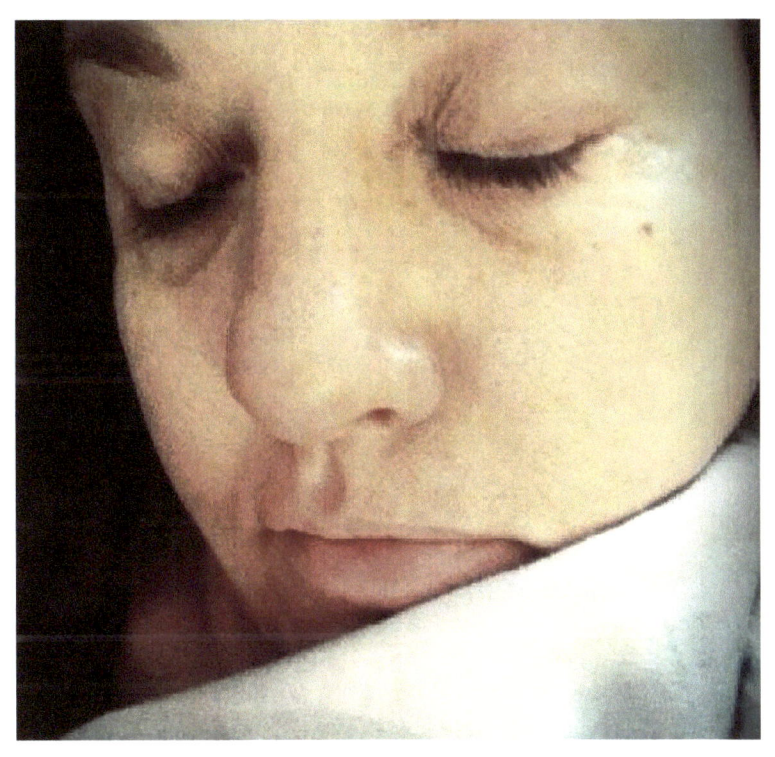

sucking
the life from me
a single mosquito

the days
when I am not myself
cocoon

mosquito merry-go-round
dizzy
shattered life
the music
plays on

useless now
these spring flowers
the seasons of our lives

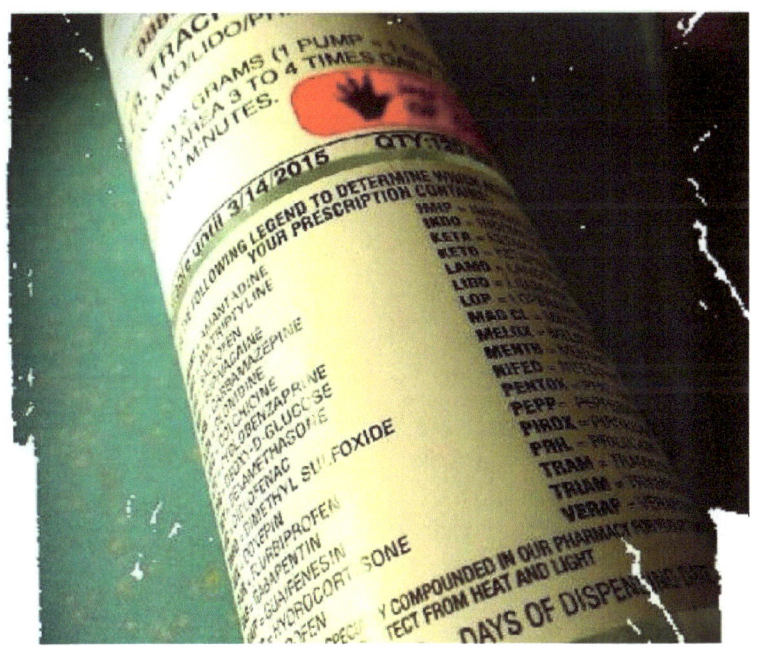

compound pharmacy
sends me
every letter
of the alphabet
still I am broken

heavily medicated
spring flowers
an overdose of rain

functioning
on narcotics
I bend
in this
spring wind

clockwork meds
I count backwards
on broken hands

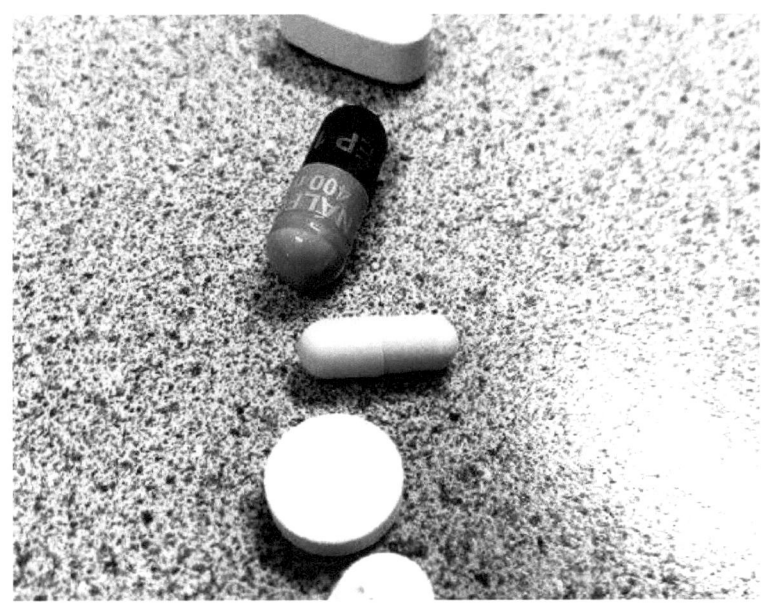

one
two
can't buckle
my
shoe

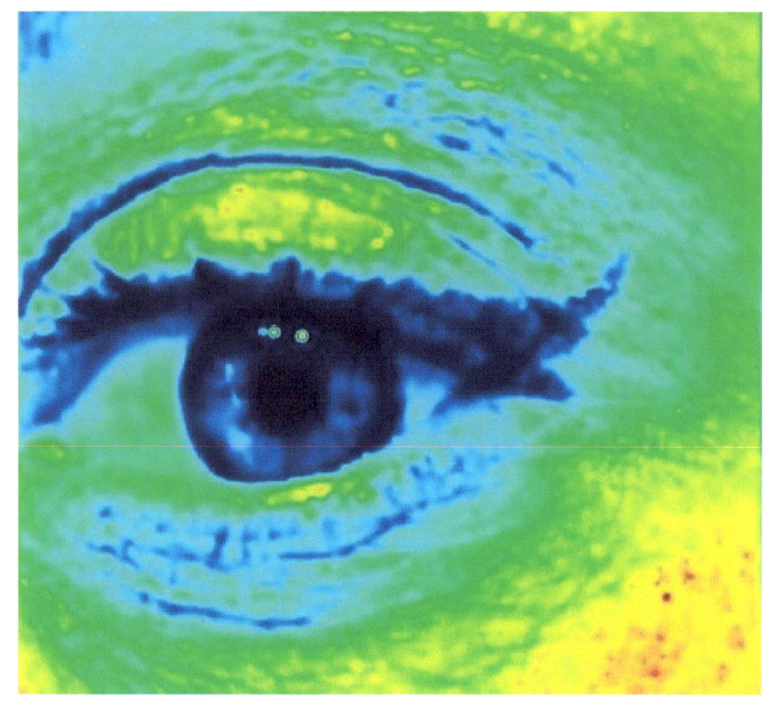

everyone happy
I've "made it"
why can't I grieve
all
I have lost?

pressing
depression
I rewind
to 1989

wishing
this pain
was "all just in my head"
I can
whisper too

not all poetry
is a beautiful
kind of pain

this crushing weight
I am
begging
for mercy

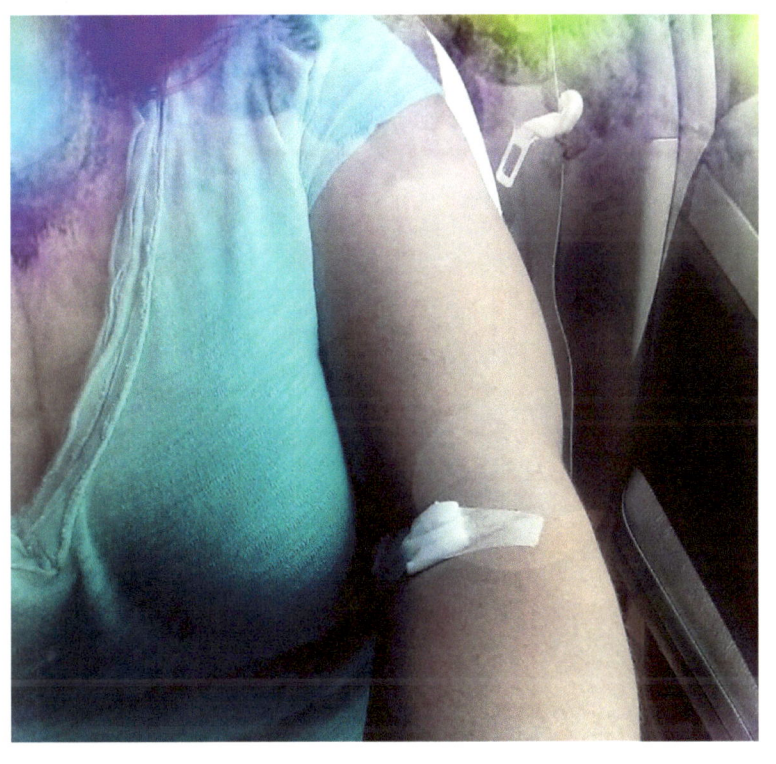

every drop
of my blood
poison
the nurse
in a HazMat suit

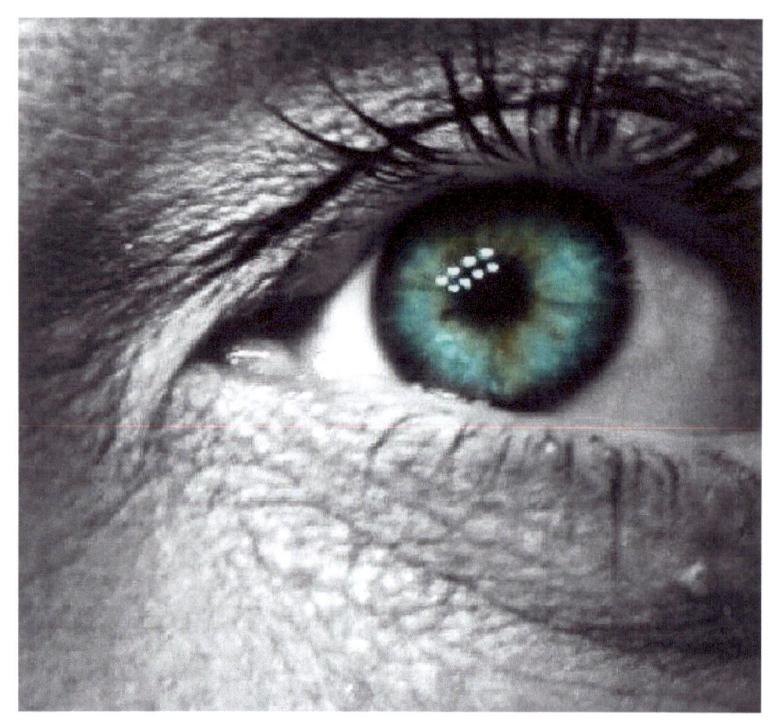

dilated haze
the pain
of what these eyes
see

all the pain meds
I want
the doctor's
blank stare

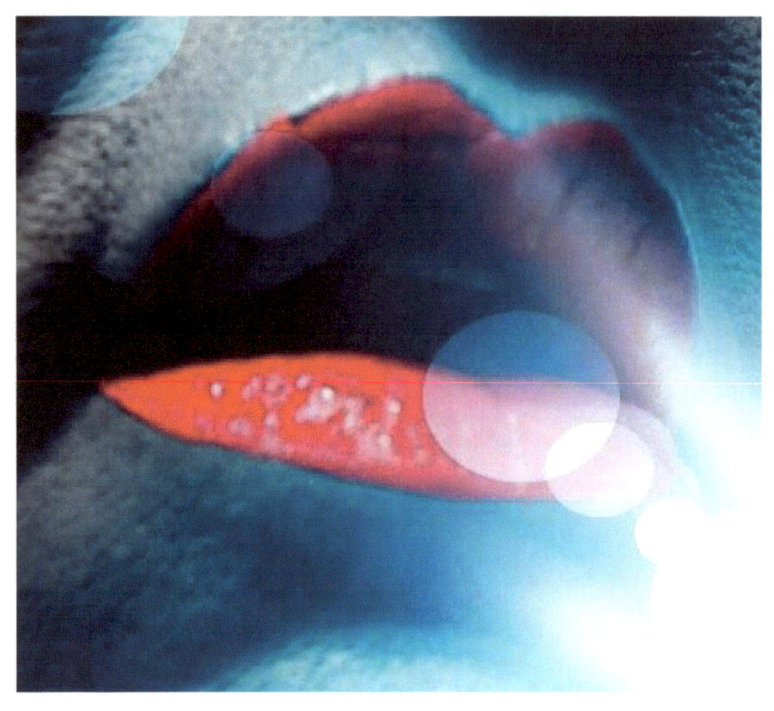

devastatingly reckless
lips laced
with morphine

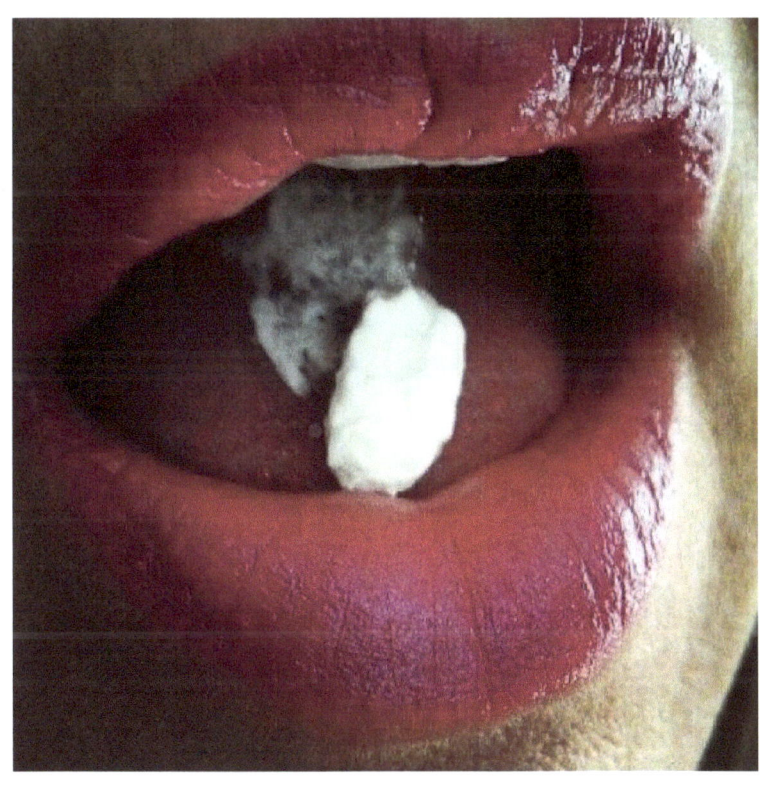

day moon
how many bitter pills
melting on my tongue

distorted view
reality
in amber
colored vials

mid day
the sky and I
sharing
the same
dark pain

morphine moondust
shattered
the sky
and I

how sleep
becomes me
last flutter
of my lashes

Acknowledgements

Morphine Moondust image from:
http://commons.wikimedia.org/wiki/File:MoonClouds.JPG

www.ingramcontent.com/pod-product-compliance
Lightning Source LLC
Chambersburg PA
CBHW041811040426
42449CB00004B/153